T. H. James

The Wooden Bowl

THE WOODEN BOWL.

Once upon a time there lived an old couple who had seen better days. Formerly they had been well to do, but misfortune came upon them, through no fault of their own, and in their old age they had become so poor that they were only just able to earn their daily bread.

One joy however remained to them. This

was their only child, a good and gentle maiden, of such wonderful beauty, that, in all that land she had no equal.

At length the father fell sick and died, and the mother and her daughter had to work harder than ever. Soon the mother felt her strength failing her, and great was her sorrow at the thought of leaving her child alone in the world.

The beauty   of the maiden
was so   dazzling
                   that it be-
                   came the
                   cause

of much
thought and anxiety to the dying mother.

She knew that in one so poor and friendless as her child, it would be likely to prove a misfortune instead of a blessing.

Feeling her end to be very near, the mother called the maiden to her bedside, and, with many words of love and warning, entreated her to continue pure, and good, and true, as she had ever been. She told her that her beauty was a perilous gift which might become her ruin, and commanded her to hide it, as much as possible, from the sight of all men.

That she   might do this the better,

the mother placed

on her daughter's head

a lacquered

wooden bowl, which she warned

her on no account to take off. The bowl
overshadowed the maiden's face, so that it
was impossible to tell how much beauty was
hidden beneath it.

After her mother's death, the poor child was indeed forlorn; but she had a brave heart, and at once

set about
earning   her living
by hard work   in the fields.
As she was never seen without

鉢／四

the wooden bowl, which indeed appeared a very funny head-dress, she soon began to be talked about, and was known in all the country round as the Maid with the Bowl on her Head.

Proud and bad people scorned and laughed at her, and the idle young

men of the village made fun of her, trying to peep under the bowl, and even to pull it off her head. But it seemed firmly fixed, and none of them succeeded in taking it off, or in getting more than a glimpse of the beautiful face beneath.

The poor girl bore all this rude usage patiently, was always diligent at her work, and when evening came, crept quietly to her lonely home. Now, one day, when she was at work in the harvest field of a rich farmer, who owned most of the land in that part, the master himself drew near. He was struck by the gentle and modest behaviour of the young girl, and by her quickness and diligence at her work.

Having watched her all that day, he was so much pleased with her, that he kept her

in work until the end of harvest. After that, winter having now come on, he took her into his own house to wait upon his wife, who had long been sick, and seldom left her bed.

Now the poor orphan had a happy home once more, for both the farmer and his wife were very kind to her. As they had no daughter of their own, she became more like the child of the house than a hired servant. And indeed, no child could have made a gentler or more tender nurse to a sick mother, than did this little maid to her mistress.

After some time the master's eldest son came home on a visit to his father and mother. He had been living in Kioto, the rich and gay city of the Mikado, where he had studied and learned much. Wearied with feasting and pleasure, he was glad to come back for a little while to the quiet home of his childhood. But week after week passed, and, to the surprise of his friends, he showed no desire to return to the more stirring life of the town.

The truth is, that no sooner had he set eyes on the Maid with the Bowl on her Head, than he was filled with curiosity to know all about her. He asked who and what she was, and why she was always seen with such a curious and unbecoming head-dress.

He was touched by her sad story, but could not help laughing at her old fancy of wearing the bowl on her head. But, as he saw day by day, her goodness and gentle manners, he laughed no more. And, one day, having managed to take   a sly peep

under the

bowl, he saw

enough of her beauty to make him

fall deeply in love with her.

From that moment he vowed that none other than the Maid with the Bowl should be his wife.   His relations, however,   would not hear of   the

match.
"No doubt the girl was all very well in her way,"

they

said, "but after all,

she was only a

servant, and no fit

mate for the son of

the house.

They had always said she was being made too much of, and would one day or another turn against her benefactors. Now their words were coming true, and besides, why did she persist in wearing that rediculous thing on her head? Doubtless to get a reputation for beauty, which most likely she did not possess. Indeed, they were almost certain that she was quite plain looking."

The two old maiden aunts of the young man were especially bitter, and never lost an opportunity of repeating the hard and unkind things which were said about the poor orphan. Her mistress even, who had been so good to her, now seemed to turn against her, and she had no friend left except her master, who would really have been pleased to welcome her as his daughter, but did not dare to say as much. The young man however, remained firm to his purpose. As for all the stories which they brought him, he gave his aunts to understand that he considered them little better than a pack of illnatured inventions.

At last, seeing him so steadfast in his determination, and that their opposition only made him the more obstinate, they were fain to give in, though with a bad grace.

A difficulty now arose where it was least to have been expected. The poor little

Maid with the Bowl on her Head upset all their calculations, by gratefully but firmly refusing the hand of her master's son, and no persuasion on his part could induce her to change her mind.

Great was the astonishment and anger of the relations. That they should be made fools of in this way was beyond all bearing. What did the ungrateful young minx expect, that her Master's son wasn't good enough for her? Little did they know her true and loyal heart. She loved him dearly, but she would not bring discord and strife into the home which had sheltered her in her poverty; for she had marked the cold looks of her mistress, and very well understood what they meant. Rather than bring trouble into that happy home she would leave it at once, and for ever. She told no one, and shed many bitter tears in secret, yet she remained true to her purpose.

Then, that night when she had cried herself to sleep, her mother appeared to her in a dream, and told her that she might, without scruple, yield to the prayers of her lover, and to the wishes of her own heart. She woke up full of joy, and, when the young man once more entreated her, she answered yes, with all her heart. "We told you so," said the mother and the aunts, but the young man was too happy to mind them. So the wedding day was fixed, and the grandest

preparations were made for the

feast. Some

unpleasant remarks were doubtless to be heard about the beggar maid and her wooden bowl, but the young man took no notice of them, and only congratulated himself upon his good fortune Now, when the wedding day had at last come, and all the company were assembled, and ready to assist at the ceremony, it seemed high time that the bowl should be removed from the head of the bride. She tried to take it off, but found, to her dismay, that it stuck fast, nor could her utmost efforts even succeed in moving it: and, when some of the relations persisted in trying to pull off the bowl, it uttered loud cries and groans as of pain.

The bridegroom comforted and consoled the maiden, and insisted that they should go on with the ceremony without more ado.

And now came the moment when the wine cups were brought in, and the bride and bridegroom must drink together the "three times three", in token that they were now become man and wife. Hardly had the bride put her lips to the *Sake* cup, when the wooden bowl burst with a loud noise, and

fell in a thousand pieces upon the floor.
And, with the bowl, fell a shower of precious
stones, pearls, and diamonds, rubies and
emeralds, which had been hidden beneath
it, besides gold and silver in abundance,
which now became the marriage portion
of the maiden.

But, what astonished the wedding guests
more even than this vast treasure, was the
wonderful beauty of the bride, made fully
known for the first time to her husband
and to all the world.

Never was there such a merry wedding,
such a proud and happy bridegroom, or
such a lovely bride.

明治廿年十一月廿二日

版權免許一八二六二號

編　者　英國人
　　　　ジェイムス夫人

出版人
東京府平民
京橋區南佐柄
本町二番地
長谷川武次郎